Poker

Poker Strategy

The Top 100 Best Ways To Greatly Improve Your Poker Game

By Ace McCloud
Copyright © 2015

Disclaimer

The information provided in this book is designed to provide helpful information on the subjects discussed. This book is not meant to be used, nor should it be used, to diagnose or treat any medical condition. For diagnosis or treatment of any medical problem, consult your own physician. The publisher and author are not responsible for any specific health or allergy needs that may require medical supervision and are not liable for any damages or negative consequences from any treatment, action, application or preparation, to any person reading or following the information in this book. Any references included are provided for informational purposes only. Readers should be aware that any websites or links listed in this book may change.

Table of Contents

Be sure to check out my website for all my Books and Audio books.

www.AcesEbooks.com

Introduction

I want to thank you and congratulate you for buying the book, "Poker: Poker Strategy: The Top 100 Best Ways To Greatly Improve Your Poker Game"

This book contains proven steps and strategies on how you can dramatically improve your poker game.

Poker has always been a favorite game of strategy and chance, but a big resurgence of popularity began in 1998 with the release of "Rounders." In this movie, Matt Damon portrayed a character who played poker in order to pay for his law degree. He wanted to win the $10,000 entrance fee to participate in the World Series of Poker to be held in Las Vegas. This movie sparked fresh interest in the next generation of poker players. All of a sudden elegant poker sets were popping up in shops just in time for Christmas and people were watching poker tournaments on TV to learn how to play the game. In the World Poker Tournament, little cameras where hidden around the table so the hands of the players could be seen by commentators describing the game to the viewers. Online poker games became an easy way to learn the game without spending a lot of money, only fueling the nation's poker fever.

Everyday people, like accountants, secretaries and students began to play in tournaments, winning large amounts of money. Some of these players even received sponsorships from various companies. Tournaments were being held all over the world.

In 2003 Chris Moneymaker, an accountant from Tennessee, decided to emulate Matt Damon in "Rounders" and began to play online in order to make the money required to enter the next World Series of Poker. He succeeded in entering the tournament, and played, winning $2.5 million and showing the world that just about anyone could win at poker.

Today, almost everyone knows a little something about the game from 21 to 5-card stud and all the way to Texas hold 'em. People play online, in family rooms or kitchens of private homes, in dorm rooms and anywhere they can find a place to play. Poker continues to be a game of strategy, but it is also a game of luck. You can have all the skill in the world, but if you don't get good cards, you had better be a good enough actor to make your opponents *think* you do.

This book isn't going to tell you what hands to play or teach you how to play the game. The 100 strategies that are included have more to do with preparation, mindset, and other psychological aspects of the game. There is much more to playing poker than getting a good hand, bluffing and computing odds. It is a cerebral game and you have to be smarter than your opponents in order to get a leg up on them and win. The strategies herein deal with making you more prepared and smarter than the average player. They teach you what to expect and what to watch for that other players may not thing about. While it won't tell you what to do to battle certain hands, it can help you become more observant and equip you to know what to do in certain situations.

Chapter 1: A Brief History of Poker

A good way to prepare, which will help your game improve, is to know where poker came from, so this is first strategy of the book.

It is a common belief that the Chinese invented the game of cards around 969 A.D. Emperor Mu-tsung and his wife were reported to have played a game called "Domino cards" with their guests on New Year's Eve.

In Egypt during the 12th and 13th centuries, games were also played using cards. During the 16th century Persians played "Treasure Cards" and began to bet on hands that consisted of 25 cards.

In Germany, the game was called "Pochen" and in France "Poque." Both came from a Spanish game developed in the 17th and 18th century called Primero. In this game, bluffing was prevalent, as was the dealing of three cards to each player. This particular game is often referred to as "Poker's Mother" because the modern day game of poker is much the same.

Poker came to North America via the Canadian French. Poque was introduced in New Orleans by Canadians. The game further spread all the way up and down the Mississippi River by riverboats that specialized in the game.

The rules to this "new" cheating game were first written down in 1834 by Jonathan H. Green. Three-card-monte had become part of the gambling circuit on riverboats. When poker offered more of a challenge, it quickly became the game of choice.

Everyone has seen old Westerns where a cheating gambler is shot during a poker game in a saloon. The game was indeed popular in the Old West. It was also a favorite game of soldiers during the Civil War. In 1875 the Joker card was introduced. Since the late 1800s, poker has been known as an American game.

Modern poker appears in many forms. The Civil War brought us Five-card draw. The state of Nevada declared this game illegal because it involved betting. California, however, turned around and touted it as a game of skill. During World War II, Seven-card stud became the popular form of poker and since them it has been the main draw of the Las Vegas casino culture.

Texas hold 'em is a relatively new game to the poker scene. It has only been around professionally since the 1970's, when it made its first appearance in the World Series of Poker.

Of course, there are many other forms of poker that can test the skill of even the most skilled player and provide a fun evening out with friends. You can now play for money online. Thousands of tournaments are available online, from all over the world.

Poker has survived the test of time and is still going strong, unlike other games that have faded away over the years. The game is here to stay and continues to evolve as new generations of players join the ranks.

Chapter 2: Get Ready To Play To Win

Preparation is essential when playing good poker. You just don't enter a game on a whim and expect to win, although a few people can do just that. However, for the rest of us who have to prepare, the following are a few things you can do to improve your chances of winning. Some may sound simplistic, but if you try them once, you will probably discover that these practices actually do make you more intuitive, more observant, and able to win more.

#2. Meditate before a game. Meditation can banish fears and make you more self-assured. Many people may say this is complete bunk. However, don't knock it until you've tried it. Our minds are endowed with a limbic system, which is the self-preservation part of the brain. The limbic system governs our fight-or-flight response. Meditation is designed to give you greater control over this part of the brain, which in turn will help you manage your fear and feel comfortable in just about any situation.

Begin your meditation by sitting comfortably and clearing your mind of any unnecessary chatter. Breathe in for a count of five, hold the breath for another five counts, and then let out your breath slowly over the space of five counts. Counting is all you need to think about and a five count is easy to pull off, even if you are in the middle of a game and get into a panic about how much money you are losing. Meditative breathing clears your mind and allows it to function more smoothly. Meditating before a game will also set you up to control your mind better during the game.

#3. Visualize Winning. This is also a part of meditation. Once you have cleared your mind, create a mental image of yourself winning a poker game. You are able to predict what your opponent is thinking and foil him every time he tries to throw you a curve. Visualize your bankroll growing and growing.

#4. Speak some affirmations. Choose some phrases that are positive in nature and that relate as specifically as possible to your game. affirmations will train your brain how to think about yourself. Write each affirmation on an index card, then cycle through these cards, speaking your affirmations aloud while meditating and while getting ready in the morning. An affirmation might say something like, "I will play aggressively to win" or "I will focus on the table and what is happening around me." You might think this could not possibly help you win more in poker, but you will be surprised at how it can help you focus and sustain mental and emotional control.

#5. Focus. Focus is imperative when playing poker. You focus on the cards you can see, you focus on the other players, you focus on your cards that no one else can see, and you must always focus on your bankroll. These are a lot of things to be focusing on simultaneously. Any technique that will increase your focus will help you improve your game.

We live in a society where distractions are everywhere. Our phones ring or tell us we have a message. Our homes are filled with electronics that can distract us on a regular basis. Those of us who have children know that they come first, but they also provide myriad distractions. It is no wonder that our attention span seems to be diminishing.

To counter all the distractions, try this exercise. Turn off all your electronics and just take in the atmosphere. Do this right before going to bed and force your mind to think of each of the things that happened throughout day, listing them in chronological order. Do not let your mind wander. Repeat this exercise for about 30 minutes every day and you will find your ability to focus will improve in just a few weeks. You will also find you are able to focus on your poker game, and for a longer period of time.

#6. Increase your focus. Another exercise that can improve your focus and lengthen your attention span begins with finding a comfortable place to sit outside. Look around at everything you can see, noting every detail. Start by looking on one side of the scene and move your eyes slowly to the other side. The only chatter in your head should be you describing what you see. Speak the phrases in your head, phrases such as, "I see an old oak with rough bark and big green leaves that have three lobes and look like the palm of a hand." "I see a robin with a brilliant red breast, brown and black feathers on his back and a yellow beak." Take it all in. Take as much time as you can for this exercise. Walk away from the area and in thirty minutes take a pen and paper and write down everything you remember. You may only remember two or three things at first, but if you keep it up, in a few weeks your focusing abilities will increase and you will be able to recall more details. This exercise will help your brain focus on the many things that happen in a poker game, so you can process them successfully.

#7. Increase your focus more. Take any old book you have laying around the house and open it to a page at random. Count the words in one paragraph. Re-count to make sure you have it right. Do this with several paragraphs. Keep your mind focused on counting and don't let it wander.

#8. Increase your focus even more. Pick up a piece of fruit. Hold it in your hand and observe it by turning it over, really looking at it. For example, observe the color of an apple. It isn't just a solid red. There are streaks of white, yellow, or green in it along with the red. Now, cut the fruit into pieces or bite into it, concentrating on the texture and the flavor. Is it crunchy or soft, tart or sweet?

Believe it or not, these focus exercises will improve your attention and make you a better poker player. Start working on them for just a few minutes each day. Gradually increase the time you spend until you feel you are adequately focusing during a game.

#9. Stop distractions during a game. If you feel yourself losing focus during a game, sit out a few hands to give your brain a rest. Stop focusing inwardly and do something that moves your body. Come back ten or fifteen minutes later and you will find your focus has been restored.

In 2014, a study was done involving both professionals and amateur poker players. Participants were hooked up to an EEG machine and their brainwaves were monitored as they played. They discovered that the more experienced players exhibited a higher level of focus and were less distracted than the amateurs. The amateurs became distracted more easily and gave in to their emotion more often, while the professionals seemed to be governed primarily by logic and intuition. Perhaps these results will encourage you to pursue the level of intense focus and logical thinking necessary to succeed at the highest levels of play.

#10. Become an optimistic person. If you are optimistic and believe you can win, you won't sabotage your success. Listen to the positive voice in your head and use your skills to win. Positive thinking works, even in poker. If you have a hard time going into a game with an optimistic attitude, make a list of the attributes you bring to the table. Maybe you are smart, you can easily calculate odds, you have great intuition, or you can bluff effectively. You have a lot going for you. Remind yourself of your strengths, repeatedly, until you begin to believe them.

#11. Enjoy the competition. Some people thrive on competition; you are lucky if you do. Just don't take it *too* far. If you are one of those people who love competition, it probably means you have an outgoing personality. Introverted people have to work on being competitive.

Competition brings out either the best or the beast in a person. In some folks, it exposes a big ego that will need to be kept in check so as not to offend others. In other people, competition stimulates an increase in positive energy. Either way, a little competition is good, just as long as you do not become a bully over it.

#12. Study books. As with almost everything in life, your poker game can improve with study. Books about poker strategies abound, both in print and electronic format. Websites contain a wealth of information, as do forums that trade information among those who actually play the game. You can find training videos on DVD and via YouTube that are very helpful. You can even find software applications that impart strategies for playing the game.

A good all-around book on Poker that includes a complete history was written by James McManus and is called *Cowboy Full: The Story of Poker*. If you want to know more about the psychology of poker, pick up *The Elements of Poker* by Tommy Angelo. This book examines life of a professional player. In it you can learn some of the best poker strategies for Hold 'em games. Most amateurs can get a good grasp on Poker from Barry Tannenbaum's *Advanced Limit Hold 'em Strategy*. Even experienced players can increase their knowledge through this book. *The Book of Bluff* by Matt Lessenger interviews professional players to learn their secrets of bluffing. David Sklansky is most well-known for explaining correlations between poker and math. His book, *The Theory of Poker*, is worth having in your arsenal.

#13. Visit Websites. The internet has a treasure trove of poker strategies to try. One site that gives you a variety of articles to peruse is "http://www.cardplayer.com/." Articles abound there, from professional players like Ed Miller, Dusty Schmidt, and Gavin Griffin. There is something on this site for everyone, from the beginner to the expert player and you can find discussions on any type of game. Another site with material for all levels of play is "http://www.pokernews.com/"; it is well worth a visit. If you search under "poker strategies" you will find hundreds of sites with worthwhile content.

#14. Join in Discussions on Poker Forums. In a poker forum you can learn from other players as they share strategies that work. It is the perfect place to pick up helpful playing advice. The "Two Plus Two Poker Forum" is a good place to start. There are multiple online forums for general poker, Texas hold 'em, tournament play, and other topics. At http://www.pokerstrategy.com/usa/ there are several forums, including general discussions, poker tools, successes, and challenges. Questions are answered on a variety of subjects at http://www.pocketfives.com/ and the dependable http://www.pokernews.com/ contains forums on current news and tournaments, among others.

#15. Obtain Training Videos. Most video sites cost you a little money for a subscription fee. In most cases, the money is well spent. The Cardrunners.com YouTube video site boasts the largest library and provides training in all games. DeucesCracked on YouTube offers a free trial membership that includes forum access. The YouTube Pokertube site provides free training for online play.

#16. Get Poker Software. "Poker Tracker" and "Holdem Manager" are two types of software that can really improve your game. They both offer free trial versions so you can test them out before parting with your hard-won cash. These programs track your hands as you play poker online. The information goes into a database and is analyzed. It reports on hands where you lose money, tracks your bets, and reports on how much you win. Either software package can be a valuable learning tool to help you play better.

Some people respond and learn better when they have a real person helping to train them. Mentors, Coaches and Gurus can make a big difference in your game.

#17. Find a Mentor. Maybe you have a buddy who always seems to win at poker. Depending on how close you are, you may want to ask him or her to be your mentor. The mentor's job is to watch you while you play. Your mentor will often play in the game with you, watching your moves from the cards he can see. Mentors also watch your facial expressions and body language, as well as what you say during a game. After the game your mentor will help you analyze your hands and tell you what you did right or wrong and help you think through the possible alternatives. He will let you know if you always squint your left eye when you have a bad hand or you wiggle your nose and sniff when you have a good hand. He will tell you things like, "I would have done this if I had that hand." A mentor takes you on, expecting no payment for services. That is why a friend or relative is a preferred way to find a mentor. You may be able to find mentors on online forums, once you get involved in them. In the future, remember how someone took the time to mentor you. You can pay back his kindness by mentoring another inexperienced player.

#18. Use a Coach. The biggest difference between a mentor and a coach is that the coach is a professional and is usually paid for his or her services. If you want to become a serious player, a coach is the way to go. A coach usually doesn't have a history with you, so he is more likely not to sugar-coat things. He will tell you what you need to know, good or bad. Coaching can be accomplished one-on-one and is usually face to face. You can email your coach the history of your hands for analysis and review. You can even meet via Skype, where you can see each other.

#19. Choose a Guru. A guru is a person with a great deal of knowledge and is someone you would like to emulate in your game. A guru personifies what you want to become. It is rare that you would ever converse with your chosen guru, but there are many ways you can learn from him. Subscribe to his blog or read his books. Watch him during tournament play to learn from his moves. Your guru is there to provide inspiration. Generally a guru will not answer direct questions or converse with you.

Watch out when choosing gurus. Always make sure their statistics match what they say is true of themselves. There are some unscrupulous people who call themselves gurus, but their stats don't stand up to what they say they can do. Many gurus make a living selling DVDs and books, so check to make sure your gurus' wares are worth having before you purchase them.

Whether you read and study, meditate, find a mentor, or choose a guru, you can only improve your game by preparing. All of these things can make you a force with which to be reckoned with at the poker table.

#20. A simple poker strategy, but a very important one, is to practice. As with anything, practice makes perfect. The more you do something, the better you are at it. Poker is no different. In fact, poker is one of those things you will never become better at *unless* you practice. You can read all the books you want, but you will never get better unless you play the game.

#21. Practice with Friends. Maybe some of your friends want to improve their poker game. Use an imaginary bankroll and discuss and analyze everyone's hand after play has completed. You will be surprised at the things you and learn from a bunch of friends sitting around a table and pretend playing.

#22. Practice Online. Playing online poker gives you some good experience and you can even try out new strategies there. Most online games are played for low stakes, so if you lose you haven't lost much. Online poker can give you valuable experience without the monetary risk of live games.

Online poker has been around since the late 1990s with Free Poker Online. Poker Planet, established in 1998, was the first site where you played for money. Online poker gave Chris Moneymaker his start when he won a spot at the table of the 2003 World Series of Poker; the spot was won in an online competition. Most online poker sites offer low stakes, so anyone can play for fun. They also provide tournaments. Online poker sites have security and watch hands for cheating and for collusion, what we call it whenever two or more players conspire together in order to win. Two players with the same IP address are not allowed to play the same game.

Be careful when you start to play online. Choose an online site that has a valid online gambling license. This keeps both the player and the site safe. You may have to download software so you can play, but it should be safe. You can even download apps on your smart phone and play. One recommended site, http://www.888poker.com/ is a popular site. The platform is user friendly and a wide range of games are offered. The site gives out bonuses and offers both case tables and tournaments with a wide variety of players. PokerStars is headquartered on the Isle of Man where there are stringent standards for online gambling. The site offers diversity in tables, lots of players, good bonuses, and large tournaments. The nice thing about online play is that you can participate any time of the day or night.

#23. Practice by visiting a casino. Head out to the casinos to practice if you have one with actual poker tables. Many casinos are moving toward machine play only, but a few still offer tables with human dealers. You will probably spend a little more money at a casino, merely because their overhead is more than online gambling sites.

If you have never been to a casino, there are certain rules to follow. If you violate the rules, you could be ejected from the casino, so pay close attention.

- Keep your chips in front of you where they can be seen and move chips you want to go into the pot to the front. Let the dealer move them into the pot.

- If you win, don't jump up and scoop the pot toward you. Let the dealer push it toward you.

- Avoid picking the cards up off the table. The dealer needs to see how many you have. If you lift them up, other players are likely to see them anyway.

- Protect your cards on the table by placing a chip on top of them. The dealer will know they are in play and will leave them alone rather than mistakenly mucking them.

- Always wait for your turn when there are many people at the table. It is really easy to get confused. If you lose track, ask the dealer to let you know when it is your turn; he will be happy to oblige.

- It is the dealer's job to keep things running smoothly. Your dealer will want to keep you happy and coming back, but if you do something unacceptable, you *will* hear about it. When you are corrected, don't take it personally. It is probably a good idea to inform the dealer, before you sit at a table, that you have very little casino experience, if that is the case.

- If you win a pot, it is customary to tip the dealer, just as you would a waitress or waiter. Dealers make most of their pay from tips. Watch what the other players are tipping and tip accordingly.

Chapter 3: Size Up The Competition

Paying attention to your opponents' body language, motions, actions, voice and other things is one way you can tell what they are thinking and sometimes predict what they will do. A smart player takes all these physical cues into consideration during a game. Watching your opponents gives you an advantage. Most people do not even know they are doing little involuntary things that reveal what they are really up to.

I highly recommend watching a YouTube video from thebestcasinoguide.com entitled "Mike Caro's Top 10 Ultimate Poker Tells." It shows how people react when they have a good hand and how to catch them.

#24. Watch your opponents and get to know them. Once you see what is normal for them, you can figure out if something looks out of place. That can mean they are trying to bluff you or they are trying some other type of deceit play. Listen to how they speak, how they move, how they sit , what they do when they have a set of good cards and win, and watch their body language right before they fold.

#25. Watch all the cards that you *can* see on the table. In most games, one or more cards are already visible and you may know what cards an opponent has decided to throw away. It is important that you pay close attention to what you *can* see, including what you have in your hand. With this knowledge you might see possibilities for straights or flush hands that your opponent could be hiding.

#26. Watch for danger signs. One sign of danger is if your opponent has bet way above normal for having a flush or a straight in her hand. Another sign of danger is if she calls out of position or if she calls every bet you make. If so, you just might have an opponent with a monster hand.

#27. Watch for Patterns. Sometimes an opponent who isn't such a good player will act in a recognizable pattern. Maybe he always checks the first round. He may call frequently and raise infrequently. If he goes outside his normal pattern, he probably has a good hand.

#28. Watch for "tells." These are things players do on a consistent basis that lets you know what they are thinking. These things are involuntary. You might have an opponent who strokes his chin, and that means he is trying to figure out how to move. If he smiles after the chin stroke however, watch out.

#29. Observe involuntary eye movements. Inexperienced players often give a quick glance toward their chips if they have a good hand. They will look away and seem to be disinterested in the game when their hand is poor. Players may even raise when they have nothing in their hand.

#30 Listen for a hum or a whistle. Some people hum or whistle when they are contented. Some inexperienced poker players also make their own kind of music at the table. If a player normally hums or whistles, especially when it is his turn, listen for when he stops. If he stops, it means he is concentrating and finds it too difficult to do two things at once. He may be trying to figure out how to get out of a sticky situation.

#31. Watch the posture of your opponents. The way players sit can give you a wealth of information about their hands. People sit straight in their chair when they have a good hand. This is second nature, because getting a good hand is exciting. Watch your own posture when you get a good hand; consciously restrain yourself from straightening up.

#32. Ignore the stare of an opponent. Being stared at is disconcerting and uncomfortable; it may feel threatening. In some cases, this is why your opponent stares at you; he wants you to become unnerved. Instead of squirming in your seat, stare back and see if he looks away. If that doesn't work, smile pleasantly and just keep playing, as you ignore the stare.

#33. Watch for the opponent who stares at his cards. Staring at the cards in your hand as if something miraculous is going to happen or change usually means a bad hand. If an opponent looks carefully at her cards, then looks quickly away and starts a cheerful conversation, she is usually trying to hide something, such as a weak hand.

#34. Watch out for obvious questions. An experienced player who asks questions he should already know is probably trying to deceive you. They know the answers and are trying to fool you with their questions. They play dumb as a form of bluff.

#35. When a player is slow to play. A player who takes a long time to respond to her turn may have much to consider because she has a poor hand. She also may be trying to make you *think* she has a bad hand, so pay attention to her bets. If she does not raise, then she probably has a bad hand.

#36. Watch for crossed arms. Crossed arms over the chest indicate a defensive posture. If the fingers of the hand also grip the upper arms, it is an indication of concern.

#37. Look for telling action before a fold. Watch what other players do right before they fold. Many will slightly or completely push away from the table before they do so. If you see a player move away from the table, you can be relatively sure he plans to fold.

#38. Smiles are telling. A normal smile involves not only the mouth, but also the cheeks and the eyes. If your opponent's eyes are not involved in the smile, you can bet she has something sinister up her sleeve and cannot be trusted.

#39. Rubbing neck, shoulders, or throat. An opponent who rubs the back of the neck, his shoulders or his throat is indicating he is frustrated, possibly by a bad hand.

#40. Rubbing hands together. Rubbing the hands together is an indication of excitement; excitement may mean she has a monster hand. In most cases, the faster she rubs her hands together, the more excitement she is feeling and the better the hand she has.

#41. Steepled Hands. When you put your hands together with palms facing each other and raise and spread your fingers with the finger tips touching, it is called steepling the hands. (Remember the old nursery rhyme, "this is the church, this is the steeple; open the doors and see all the people?") Steepling is an indication of self-assurance and the higher the steeple, the more self-assured is the player.

#42 Covering the mouth. You might be able to tell if an opponent is bluffing if he covers his mouth with his hand. The subconscious mind is trying to keep deception from coming out of the mouth.

#43. Have patience. Avoid becoming aggravated by plays or by the delays of other players. Don't play into or be affected by others' actions. Keep yourself cool and composed and don't change your emotions. Should another player lose her composure, don't give in, but keep yours.

Body language can provide useful tells, but remember you also have them. Take care to keep your own movements in check. Also be aware that other players know about tells and might be purposely using theirs as a deception. They may steeple their hands when they have a bad hand, just because they know people will take it to mean they have a good hand.

Learn the psychology of the game. What is the reason you are playing poker? Is it to have a good time with friends or family or is it to win and make money? You play differently, depending on your answer to this question. You might take it easy on your friends. When you play poker, it will be necessary to deceive your friends, hide things from them, and possibly even to wipe them off the table. The whole idea is to keep your opponents unbalanced and guessing by being unpredictable. Make sure you are prepared for the emotional side of the game. If you go for blood, a friend might become offended. Is it worth it to risk a friendship over a game of poker? You may not want to make an enemy, at least not this way.

Then again, your friends might encourage you to excel at the game. In that case, they will cheer with you when you beat them and are less likely to take it personally.

Chapter 4: The Best Poker Strategies

The following tips explain all kinds of important things that happen during a poker game. All of these – from your position on the table to calculating odds – can be used to help you to win.

#44. Get a good position at the table. Your position can make or break your poker game. Position is the order in which players are seated around the table. Those who have early positions – who play early in the playing order – need to have strong hands in order to raise or call. Those in the later positions have the advantage, because they can observe how each opponent acts and get an idea of opponents' hands before it is their turn to play.

Go for a later position. The best spot is right in front of the dealer. Those in an early position have to act before they have an inkling of what other players might have in their hands. They must raise or fold blindly. Learn more about how position can affect your game in this video from The Poker Network entitled "Poker Strategy Positions (part 1) Poker Tips for Cash Poker."

#45. Learn to Bluff. Bluffing and deception are a major part of poker, but there are players who make good money even without it. You have to know when forms of deception will work and when they won't. A bluff consists of making your opponents believe something different from what you are actually going to do. This tactic is most often used when you have a weak hand and want others to think you have a winning hand; your objective is to cause your opponents to fold. If successful, you will win the pot with a terrible hand.

There are two different types of poker bluff. The **pure bluff** is a bet when the bluffer has no chance of winning. The bluffer wants opponents to fold because they think he has a good hand. **Semi-bluffing** is used in games with multiple rounds. The bluff comes in a round where the bluffer has a bad hand that could improve as play progresses. The bluffer can win if other players fold right away, or by getting a card that makes their hand better.

#46. Save your bluffs for when you know they can be successful. Amateurs seem to think they *always* have to bluff, but that is not so. You run the risk of losing your bluff if you bluff too consistently.

#47. Check your position before bluffing. Bluffs are much more successful when you are in one of the last positions on the table. The best place is to be sitting last or second to the last in a round. This gives you ample time to see what everyone else has done so you can formulate a workable bluff.

#48. Bluffs work better when only a few players are in the game. If you have to wait a while for the turn to come back to you, your bluff might backfire. Wait until most of the players have folded and there are only a few left.

#49. Practice your poker face. A poker face is devoid of any emotion and shows only casual movements. Avoid smiling too much or opening your eyes wide. Look in a mirror and actually practice holding your poker face.

#50. Slow Play. Slow play is almost the opposite of bluffing. In this case the player bets in a weak manner while holding a good hand. He bets just enough to stay in the game. This convinces opponents with worse hands to either call or raise the bet and not to fold. This tactic has the benefit of increasing the pot. However, in some venues, slow play is considered bad form, so don't use it too frequently.

You should probably become familiar with some of the terms of play in poker so you know what is going on.

- **Check**. No bet is made, but the player wants to stay in the game with the right to call or to raise later. This can only be done if the player has not yet made an opening bet.

- **Open**. This is the first bet made in the first round of play.

- **Call**. This consists of matching a bet that was made by a previous player in the current round. For example, the player two seats before you makes a $5 bet and the next player folds. You call, matching the $5 and adding the equivalent chips to the pot.

- **Raise**. This occurs when a player increases the previous bet. In the above example you could raise the bet to $10 instead of $5. This puts more money in the pot and makes other players think you have a strong hand.

- **Fold**. When a player drops out of the game, he folds. Any money he has bet is forfeit.

#51. Check at the right time. Check when you have a questionable hand. There is no sense betting on a hand that can't win, but if there is a chance you can make a better hand with a yet-to-be-seen draw or a community card, use your check.

#52 Use the check-raise trick. To do a check-raise, check when you have your turn and wait for the next player to bet. Once he or she does, you immediately raise. By checking in the first place, you have deceived other players into thinking you have a weak hand. A check-raise puts more money in the pot and marks you as unpredictable. If your opponent has a less than good hand, he is likely to fold and you will have eliminated a player.

Only use the check raise when you are in an early position on the table. You must check before your opponents play for it to work. Also, never use check-raise if you believe your opponent has a good hand. While this tactic will put more money in the pot, you may also lose. Use the check-raise only with small pots. Your opponent will probably call in order to see the next card drawn; if the bet is too big in relation to the pot size, your odds of winning will decrease. Be careful about using a check-raise too often because it is a bit underhanded and might even be an illegal move in some games.

#53. Learn when to call. Call during a drawn hand so you can get a look at other, newer cards. This gives you a better idea of the odds.

#54. Ask yourself questions to make sure your betting is appropriate. When it comes time to make a bet, first ask yourself a few questions and avoid any quick decisions you might regret later.

- The first question you should ask is "Why should I make this bet?" Is there a good reason? A good reason would be that you have a good hand. You've calculated the odds of winning and it looks good. You are in a good position at the table and you can predict what other players may have. If you can't answer this question with one of those answers, think twice about betting.

- The second question is "What should happen after I make this bet? You must consider if your opponents will raise or call and what you could do if either occurs.

- The third question is "What will opponents think I'm trying to do if I make this bet?" Maybe they will think you are bluffing. Maybe they will think you have a good hand. What you communicate to your opponents is something to consider before jumping into a bet.

This process only takes a few seconds to achieve and will save you money and time. Consider all options before betting. The longer you play and more experience you gather, the better you will understand the importance of this step.

#55. Learn when to raise. If you have a good hand, raise instead of calling. This will put more money in the pot for you to win.

#56. Raise in order to thin out the field. Raising can often drive less aggressive players out of the game, but be sure you have a good hand before you try this. Players who continually check are hoping to get a glance at cards that might improve their hand; if you raise, others can't see those cards. The more opponents you eliminate from the game, the fewer people there are to fight for the pot.

#57. Raise to get information. Raising can give you some useful information about your opponents. If you really don't have a good hand, raise with great caution, keeping in mind that this tactic will only work if your opponent calls. If she does not raise, you can pretty much bet that she does not have a good hand.

#58. Raise to get a free card. During a drawing hand, when you are able to get new cards from the dealer, raise. Your opponent likely will call the bet and during the next betting round, he will check. This gives you a chance to improve your hand by getting a free card.

#59. Try a re-raise. Re-raising can be dangerous and expensive, but if you enjoy a challenge, go for it. If you re-raise at the right time, it can be a satisfying situation. Think about your opponent who will call an extra raise, and then make sure your hand is strong before you do the re-raise.

#60. Don't get over zealous. Even if you are positive your opponent is bluffing, don't get over zealous by raising and re-raising. You may be wrong and will ultimately suffer if your opponent really does have a monster hand

#61. Learn when to fold. Force yourself to fold sometimes when you have a strong hand. If you are on a winning streak, it is sometimes a good thing to fold, especially when there isn't much in the pot anyway. Opponents won't call or raise if they think you are going to win all the time. Some players refuse to fold ever; that can be an expensive practice.

#62 Make a goal. Your goal may be to force your opponents to fold. In this case, you would bet low amounts; as low as you can. This allows you to save money. Instead of betting the entire pot, just go half to 2/3rds. You risk losing fewer chips when play it this way, especially if your opponent calls.

#63. Control the hand. In some cases you want other players to know you have a good hand, so keep on calling and raising. Other players with good hands will think yours is better and eventually fold, following all the players who didn't have good hands. You will be left to claim the pot.

#64. Watch your stack. Your stack is the chips you use for betting. If you are running low, fold instead of calling or raising. Wait until you have a sure thing to bet on so you can replenish your stack.

Winning at poker takes luck, but it also takes some skill. One thing you must learn in order to be a successful player is to calculate the odds. Odds are the percentage chance you have to win the pot. The pot is, of course, all the money bet during a game; in the end, it goes to the winner. Calculating the odds lets you decide if the pot is worth going for or not and whether to stay in a game or fold.

#65. Calculate your outs. In order to calculate the odds, you must first decide how many outs you have. Outs are specific cards that help you win a hand. For example, you have a king of diamonds in your hand. The dealer lays down a 6 of clubs, an ace of spades, a queen of diamonds and an ace of diamonds.

You know there are 4 diamonds on the table. Each deck of cards has four suits: hearts, diamonds, spades and clubs. Each suit consists of thirteen cards from ace to 2. On the table you see four diamonds, so you subtract 13-4+9=9. You have 9 outs.

#66. Use outs to calculate odds. Each deck has 52 cards. In your hand you hold, as described above, two cards including the king of diamonds and on the table there are four cards including two diamonds. That makes six cards (two in your hand + four on the table =6). That means there are now 46 cards in the deck (52-6=46). There are 37 remaining cards that could cause you to lose and 9 that will help you win. Divide 9 into 36 and you get a 4:1 ration (36/9=4). You are currently four times more likely to lose than you are to win. The 4:1 ratio is your odds and, frankly, they aren't very good right now.

#67. Decide if the pot is worth playing from your odds. We will say the pot has $90 in it. Your opponent bets $10. That puts $100 in the pot. If you want to stay in the game, you must at least contribute $10. If you win the pot, you will make $40 total dollars after what you have put into it. Is your hand worth risking more money? If it is a good hand, the answer is yes. If the hand is bad, it is better to fold.

All this might sound confusing, but once you understand how to calculate outs and odds, you can do it in a few seconds. Practice when playing with friends or playing online. Do an online search for a poker odds chart. These charts will help your calculations until you can do it all in your head.

The following are a few online strategies. Playing online offers different challenges from playing in person. You can't see your opponent, so you kind of have to guess what he is thinking.

#68. Watch online players who call right away. An online player who responds with a call almost immediately after a bet is made, without even thinking about it, might be trying to convince you she has a good hand when she doesn't. She are trying to say she has a strong hand and is hoping you will be surprised by her quick response and fold, instead of turning around and betting back into her.

#69. Watch online players who use the "in turn" button. Players who use the "in turn" button instead of the check or fold button are most likely playing multiple tables at one time and don't have time to devote themselves to the table you are on. It might be that the stakes are lower here or the pot doesn't have much money in it. You can use that to your advantage because they are not paying attention.

#70. Watch for online players who take forever to check. If they are going to check, they should be able to know that pretty quickly and without too much hesitation. Their strategy in taking a great deal of time to do it is to convince you not to bet so they can see the next card drawn without putting up any money.

Chapter 5: What's Your Style?

In poker, players come in four major styles. Everyone knows how to identify an aggressive player. They are the ones who make their presence known in the game. Passive players are the ones you hardly even know are there. You have players who play hands no matter if they are good or bad and you have players who hardly play at all and you wonder why they are even out to play poker.

A video from Poker Stars called "Poker Playing Styles" will give you an idea of the basic playing styles, and what tactics you might want to adopt with these types of players.

The first thing to determine in order to size up your opponent's style is to figure out if he is a tight or a loose player.

Tight players limit themselves to a small percentage of hands and only play the best ones they get. A loose player will play a wide variety of hands and almost always participates in hands, regardless of the quality of his cards.. Being a tight or loose player has nothing to do with the manner in which you play, but it does affect *what* you play.

The next thing to determine is whether your opponents are passive or aggressive.

A passive player avoids confrontation and fears losing. She checks more often and watches how many chips she is down. An aggressive player thrives on confrontation and has no fear of risk. She raises more plays than she calls and is not afraid of losing her chips.

The four styles of poker are:

- Tight-passive

- Tight-aggressive (TAG)

- Loose-passive

- Loose-aggressive (LAG)

The signs of a tight-passive player are that he does not play many hands and he calls frequently. If he does not fold, you will be safe betting this player has a good hand, because good hands are all he will play. Tight passive players have a hard time against an aggressive player and they are very easy to bluff.

A tight-aggressive (TAG) player also does not play many hands and only plays with a good hand. When these players *do* get that good hand, they play strongly, waiting patiently for the best time to bet and make their deadly strike. Other players tend to avoid confrontation when these guys become aggressive, because it means they do have a good hand. Tight-aggressive players rarely fold under pressure.

Loose-passive players play a variety of hands but they do not usually take chances. They will call raises just to see what cards are laid on the table. The loose-passive player lets everyone else take all the risk and are hard to bluff. Because they call all the time, it is easy to win more money in the pot from a loose-passive player. Other players will know and take advantage of this trait.

Loose-aggressive (LAG) players tend to raise and re-raise and will bet in most cases. They are very hard to read, because they play almost all hands. They use chips as pressure tactics and bluff frequently. The loose-aggressive player looks like he is raising for no good reason; that makes this type of player highly unpredictable.

So, what is the best type of player to be in order to win? Most say an aggressive style wins most of the time because the player's actions are unpredictable. An aggressive player will mix things up so no one knows what he is thinking and planning.

The aggressive style wins the most often. You have to decide whether you want to only play a percentage of the time and stay tight or play all the time and be loose. The loose-passive style is probably the worst playing option, but if you want to add unpredictability to your game persona, you can start out playing in this style and change to another style partway through a game.

#71. Practice aggressive playing. If you want to be more aggressive, you will need to practice. Set up a game with friends and explain what you are doing. You will probably find that they are okay being used as guinea pigs and might find it interesting. Try a tight-aggressive style and only play with a strong hand. Ask your opponents what they think of this type of play after a few hands. Switch to loose-aggressive and play almost every hand.

The following few tips will help you play against different styles. You do need to be able to play using each style. However, equally important is knowing how to play effectively against your opponents' styles.

#72. When you play against a loose player, call frequently. Let the other players drive up the pot.

#73. When you are up against a tight player, raise or re-raise frequently, as this also increases the money in the pot.

#74. Playing against a tight-passive player. If a drawing hand is on the current flop, use a check. A tight-passive player hardly ever bets, so you will see the next cards drawn without having to pay for them.

#75. When you are playing against a loose-passive player, only bet if you have a good hand. Avoid bluffing, because a loose-passive player will call most of the time. If the player bets, fold unless you have a good hand. If he bets, he *does* have a good hand, no question about it.

#76. When you are up against a tight-aggressive player, if he bets pre-flop, fold unless you have a best starting hand and then play aggressively and re-raise if you have two aces, two kings or two queens. If you play out of position with a tight-aggressive player and have a very good hand, check on the flop. A tight-aggressive player will bet even if he does not hit the flop.

#77. When you play against a loose-aggressive player, raise before the flop if you have a strong hand. This will isolate your loose-aggressive opponent. If the loose-aggressive opponent has a better position on the table, wait to raise until she plays again.

Strive to play in the tight-aggressive style in order to win, but remember there are always going to be other players playing with this style.

Chapter 6: Avoid These Mistakes

Every poker player makes a mistake now and then. When you first start to play the game, expect to make many mistakes. That is how you learn, but hopefully it won't be an expensive learning process. The only way you stop making big mistakes is to become an experienced player. The following are some common mistakes every player makes and, hopefully, learns to avoid.

#78. Avoid playing when drunk. Beer is a common beverage at poker games, there is nothing wrong with that. However, watch how much you drink. You need a clear head in order to pay attention to your cards and all the possibilities they bring. Even a few beers or other alcoholic drinks can affect your focus. You might feel more relaxed, but you also may miss important information when you drink too much. Limit yourself to two drinks and sip soft drinks the rest of the time.

#79. Avoid playing when in a bad or angry mood. Nothing is worse than going into a game with a negative attitude. Poker is an emotional game and you are doing yourself no good by playing in a negative state of mind. Angry and depressed people often are distracted and irrational. If you become angry at a fellow player, take a break from the game and get yourself under control before you come back. Besides, revenge is easier accomplished from a clear head.

#80. Do not play every hand. This is a big mistake that inexperienced players all do. You do not have to play every hand. Do not play especially if you have a bad hand and there is no way it can improve. If you do play, you will likely lose money. In most cases, if you play more than half the hands that are dealt, you are playing too many. You need to think a little more about which hands are good and which aren't. Never try to convince yourself you might get a good card along the way. If there is no way your hand can improve, then fold and get out of the hand.

#81. Avoid bluffing too much. Bluffing is a part of the poker game, but just like you have to know when to fold, you must know when to bluff. Use your intuition and watch the other players. If you bluff all the time, you will be known as a bluffer and it is kind of like the boy who called wolf. After awhile you won't be taken seriously.

#82. Never bluff when you know you will not win. Inexperienced players often bluff rather than fold when their hand is weak. An experienced player will catch them right off. It is not worth the risk. Bluffing experience players is a big mistake. Expert players are good at seeing chinks in other players' armor and they will find yours. Your bluff will be called and if you don't have a good hand, you will lose.

#83. Avoid playing in games with higher limits than you can afford. Do not try to impress anyone by playing a high limit game with low resources or

29

experience. Make sure you are ready for those high stake games and understand how to play, how to read your opponents and how to stay cool. You may be tempted to try a table with high stakes, but it is better to play with lower limits and win than to be greedy and play high limits and loose.

#84. Pick a game that matches your skills. Have you ever played Texas Hold 'em or have you only played stud games before? Make sure the game you get into is one you are familiar with. If you aren't very good at the hold 'em games, wait to play for money until you get better and learn the game. Stick to what you know and you will avoid losing money.

#85. Limit your bankroll before you enter a game. Your bankroll is the amount of money you bring to the game to play. It includes any buy in or regular bets. Avoid using up the entire bankroll all at once. Hold some of it back to get you through loses. This will give you a reserve when you need it.

#86. Don't ignore the size of your stack. Always watch the size of your stack or bankroll. Don't let it get too low. Your stack is right out there where everyone can see it and if other players see that it is getting low, they may think they can take advantage of you. They will bet larger amounts than they think you can afford. Buy more chips before your stack gets too low.

#87. Avoid betting predictability. Avoid betting the same way every time. This makes you predictable and a bad player. Varying your bets makes your opponents less likely to figure you out. Give them a surprise once in awhile so you are less readable.

#88. Don't bet on a low pot. Inexperienced players will not figure odds or pay attention to the money in the pot. It is not worth risking more money on a pot where you are not going to make money. There is no sense in insisting on winning. Just fold and lose a little bit instead of losing a lot.

#89. Listen to your instincts. If the situation feels bad, it usually *is* bad. Go with your feelings and fold instead of playing and regretting it. Everyone has intuition, so learn how to trust yours. You might see something out of place during a game. It might be an unusual movement, uncharacteristic language, or dead silence. Open yourself up to your instinct and intuition. You will be surprised how this will improve your game.

#90. Do not rush deciding how to play. Take a look at your hand, at the odds and never rush to make a decision. Rushed plays usually do not end well.

#91. Don't depend on suited cards. Some players fool themselves into thinking they are going to win with a hand that contains many cards of one suit, but getting a flush is hard to do; even if you do have a flush, someone else may still have a better hand. Suited hands rarely pay off unless, of course, you have a royal flush. But how many times does that happen?

Playing frequently will help you learn what and what not to do in a game. Experienced players make fewer mistakes than inexperienced players, but there is always a chance of being off your game, once in a while. If you do make a mistake, don't beat yourself up about it. Learn from the situation and make yourself a better player.

Chapter 7: Winning Hands & Winning Tactics

It is important to know the winning hands in poker. It is also important to know the statistics of getting those winning hands. A deck of cards has 52 total cards in it. Within these 52 cards the total unique hands that can be dealt in Five-card stud poker is 2,598,960. This is the number we use in developing statistics for each type of hand.

The best hand to draw is a royal flush. This is a straight that runs from 10 to ace of a matching suit. An example would be the Ace of hearts, king of hearts, queen of hearts, jack of hearts and 10 of hearts. If you have this hand dealt to you, you must be the luckiest person on earth. The chance of this happening is 4 in 2,598,960 or 0.00015%. It's a good thing there are multiple rounds in poker. There are always more chances to receive a royal flush, but it doesn't happen very often.

Next in line is a straight flush. This is when you have any five consecutive cards of the same suit, like a 5, 6, 7, 8, and 9 of spades. The chance of this happening in a deal is 32 in 2,598,960 or 0.00123%, still not good odds.

Four of a kind is the next best type of hand. An example of this would be having an ace of hearts, ace of diamonds, ace of spades, ace of clubs and some other card, say, the king of hearts. Here the king will determine who wins, if someone else has four of a kind. In this case, the king is called the kicker; because the king is the highest card, it will win. The statistics of getting this kind of hand are a little better, at 624 in 2,598,960 or 0.0240%.

A full house comes next in ranking; it consists of 3 of the same rank cards plus two of the same rank. The highest full house you can get is three aces and two kings, which is better than three kings and two aces. But you can have other combinations of full-house hands, like three jacks and two queens or three 10s and two 5s. The probability of being dealt a full house is 3,744 in 2,598,960 or 0.144%, still not very good odds.

A flush comes next. It consists of any five cards from the same suit; they do not have to be consecutive. An example would be a king, 9, 8, 4, and 2 of clubs. The king is the highest rank, so if an opponent also has a flush with the highest rank being a jack, you would still win. The odds for being dealt a flush are 5,112 in 2,598,960 or 0.353%.

A straight is made up of five consecutive cards of any suit, such as the 10 of clubs, the 9 of diamonds, the 8 of hearts, the 7 of diamonds and the 6 of clubs. If an opponent also has a straight, the highest card wins. If you have a 10 of clubs and your opponent has a jack of hearts. He would win. The chance of being dealt a straight is much better than the others at 9,180 in 2,598,960 or 0.353%.

Three of a kind is next on the totem pole. You need to have three cards of the same rank, such as three kings. The best possible three-of-a-kind combination is three aces, a king, and a queen. This will beat other three-of-a-kind combinations, like three 10s, an 8 of spades and 9 of diamonds. The probability of being dealt this type of hand is much greater at 54,912 in 2,598,960 or 2.11%. This brings us up into the whole numbers in our statistical reckoning.

Two pair is next, which means you have two cards of the same rank and another two cards of the same rank. The best hand you can have for this is two aces, two kings and a queen. This will win over two queens, two jacks and a 10. The chance of being dealt this hand is 123,552 in 2,598,960 or 4.75%.

One pair is any two ranked cards, such as two aces, or two tens. The best possible hand with one pair is two aces of any suit, plus any king, queen or jack. You can make do with your pair being any rank cards, although it is hard to win with this hand. The chances of being dealt one pair is very good, at 1,098,240 in,598,960 or 42.26%.

The bottom of the probability hierarchy is the high card; the probability of getting this on the first deal is 1,303,560 or 50.16%. You may have the ace of hearts, the king of spades, the queen of diamonds, the 9 of clubs and the five of diamonds. Your ace is the high card and not likely to get you anywhere, unless you can bluff really well.

These statistics can help you put everything into perspective. They show why it is important to have an arsenal of strategies when you go into a poker game. The following are a few more strategies that might help you gain the upper hand in different poker games.

#92. Use a Steal-play strategy. This play is most often done in Five-card draw situations and it puts a little more money in your hand. If you have a flush or a straight, three of a kind, or two pairs, and you are one of the last people to act on the table before a card drawn, with no one entered into the pot yet, make a raise in order to win the blinds or antes. You won't win a lot, but you will perform a bit of deception that will give you a little more money to work with.

#93. Fool opponents into thinking you have a good hand. In Five-card draw games, most people will draw three cards when they have a pair or they will draw two cards when they have three of a kind. They will only draw one when they have two pairs or four cards that can make a flush or a straight. This is predictable. Fool your opponents by only drawing one card. They will think you actually do have a flush or a straight. Draw only two cards when you have a pair or a trash hand and your opponents will think you have three of a kind.

#94. Play tight-aggressive style in Texas hold 'em. Only play decent hands in Texas Hold 'em and when you do play, push the action by betting and raising. Avoid checking and calling. Your opponent will most likely fold if you are this aggressive, but you will only win if you have a good hand or can bluff like no other.

#95.   Watch game progression.   This is true in almost any game, but important for Texas Hold 'em games. You can always start out with a really good hand and end up losing. You must re-evaluate your hand, especially the two hole cards three times during the game.   You should re-evaluate your hand after seeing the flop, at the turn, and at the river.   Keep an eye on your cards to ascertain if they are still in good standing or not. Don't assume they are.

#96.   Bet after the river.   In Texas hold 'em, the river card is the most important of all, because you are getting towards the end of the game when the pot is won. Watch the player who goes before you; if he bets conservatively, make a large bet. That usually will cause him to fold. If he makes a large initial bet and you have a really good hand, call and go all-in.

#97.   Strive to go either low or high in Omaha hi/low.   In Omaha hi/lo, you are looking for hands consisting of either four low cards or four high cards or two of each. The best hand to get is one that you can go either way with, one that includes an ace.

#98.   Strive to go either low or high in Stud hi/low.   The same advice applies to stud hi/low, but don't try to go for a low if your cards are not suited. If you would like to go high, start with a pair of aces or three cards that can lead to a royal flush.

#99.   Switch Tables in Online poker.   Switch your tables every two to three rounds or games in order to keep from getting bored and complacent and to keep opponents from figuring out your style.   In online play, you can participate in more than one table at a time.   Each table is displayed in a separate window. Paying attention to multiple screens and up to four sets of cards is a task, but if you can do it. go for it. Just don't take on more than you can handle.

#100.   This is the Most Important Poker Strategy.   It is probably the most important strategy of all.   Once the cards are dealt to you, take them, ruminate over them, and create a strategy for playing those cards.   Do you have a pair? Work with that. Do you have three cards that can be built into a straight or a flush? Work with that. Don't play just to play, if you have nothing but a high card that isn't very high. You don't have to play super conservatively, but you do have to make sense.   Betting on a hand that has a pair of threes alone is ridiculous. There are other, hands to come. Fold and wait for something better to come along. Don't play just to get back at someone, hoping to make him squirm in his seat; that rarely works out well. Don't play because you are bored. If you have a bad hand, you will continue to be bored. Play good hands and fold on bad ones. If you play over 50% of your hands you are either a lucky god or a fool.

Conclusion

I hope this book was able to help you increase your knowledge of poker strategies. You now have 100 different strategies and have increased your insight on what makes a winning hand and a winning player in poker. Poker is a game of luck, but it is also a game of psychology. This book has included both types of aspects, from how to play your cards to discerning what makes your opponent tick. It gives you advice on what you can deduce from your opponents' actions and the cards you can see. It helps you figure out what your opponent is trying to tell you, both consciously and unconsciously.

Your next step is to apply these strategies in real live play, either in person or online. Practice the methods in this book and you should be able to win, win, and win more in whatever venue you choose. Some of these strategies sound simple and a few may be something you never have considered before. However, things like the meditation techniques are common player strategies; if you try them (even when no one else is around) you will find they really do make a difference. They just might turn your game around for the better.

Finally, if you discovered at least one thing that has helped you or that you think would be beneficial to someone else, be sure to take a few seconds to easily post a quick positive review. As an author, your positive feedback is desperately needed. Your highly valuable five star reviews are like a river of golden joy flowing through a sunny forest of mighty trees and beautiful flowers! *To do your good deed in making the world a better place by helping others with your valuable insight, just leave a nice review.*

My Other Books and Audio Books
www.AcesEbooks.com

Peak Performance Books

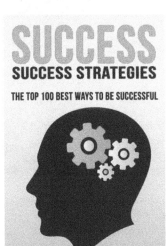

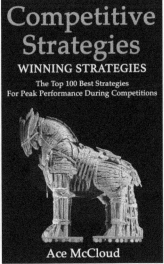

Health Books

ULTIMATE HEALTH SECRETS

HEALTH

Strategies For Dieting, Eating Healthy, Exercising, Losing Weight, The Mediterranean Diet, Strength Training, And All About Vitamins, Minerals, And Supplements

Ace McCloud

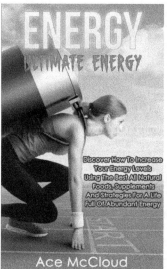

ENERGY
ULTIMATE ENERGY

Discover How To Increase Your Energy Levels Using The Best All Natural Foods, Supplements And Strategies For A Life Full Of Abundant Energy

Ace McCloud

RECIPE BOOK

The Best Food Recipes That Are Delicious, Healthy, Great For Energy And Easy To Make

Ace McCloud

MASSAGE THERAPY

TRIGGER POINT THERAPY
ACUPRESSURE THERAPY
Learn The Best Techniques For Optimum Pain Relief And Relaxation

Ace McCloud

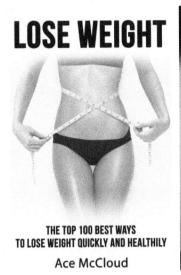

LOSE WEIGHT

THE TOP 100 BEST WAYS TO LOSE WEIGHT QUICKLY AND HEALTHILY

Ace McCloud

FATIGUE
OVERCOME CHRONIC FATIGUE

Discover How To Energize Your Body & Mind So That You Can Bring The Energy & Passion Back Into Your Life

Ace McCloud

Be sure to check out my audio books as well!

Happiness

The Top 100 Best Ways To Feel Good & Be Happy

Ace McCloud

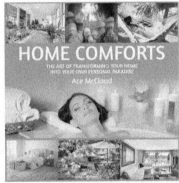

HOME COMFORTS

THE ART OF TRANSFORMING YOUR HOME INTO YOUR OWN PERSONAL PARADISE

Ace McCloud

MOTIVATION

MASTER THE POWER OF MOTIVATION TO PROPEL YOURSELF TO SUCCESS

Ace McCloud

FACEBOOK

THE TOP 100 BEST WAYS TO USE FACEBOOK FOR BUSINESS, MARKETING & MAKING MONEY

Ace McCloud

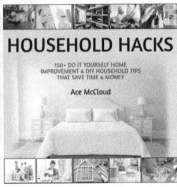

HOUSEHOLD HACKS

150+ DO IT YOURSELF HOME IMPROVEMENT & DIY HOUSEHOLD TIPS THAT SAVE TIME & MONEY

Ace McCloud

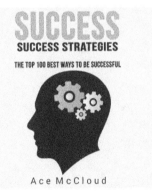

SUCCESS
SUCCESS STRATEGIES

THE TOP 100 BEST WAYS TO BE SUCCESSFUL

Ace McCloud

Check out my website at: www.AcesEbooks.com for a complete list of all of my books and high quality audio books. I enjoy bringing you the best knowledge in the world and wish you the best in using this information to make your journey through life better and more enjoyable! **Best of luck to you!**

CPSIA information can be obtained
at www.ICGtesting.com
Printed in the USA
LVHW06*1444090718
583153LV00010B/88/P